British Woodies

from the 1920s to the 1950s

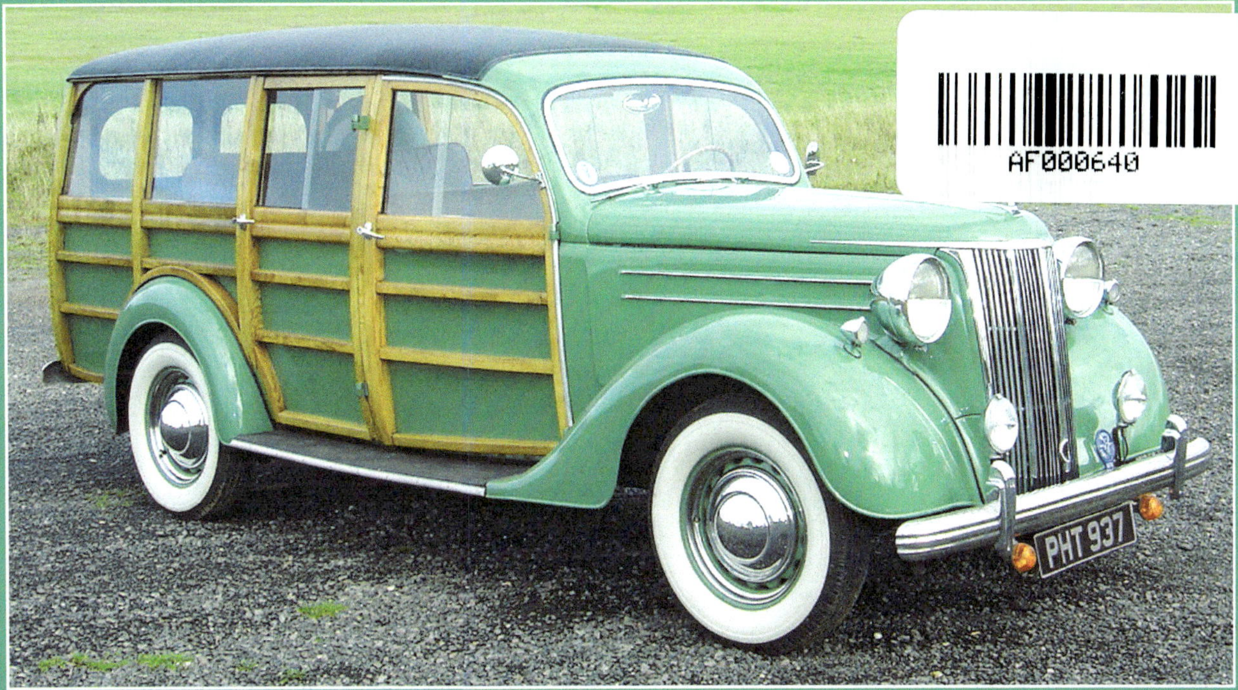

Those were the days ...

VELOCE

Also from Veloce Publishing –

Those Were The Days ... Series

Alpine Trials & Rallies 1910-1973 (Pfundner)
American 1/2-ton Pickup Trucks of the 1950s (Mort)
American 1/2-ton Pickup Trucks of the 1960s (Mort)
American 'Independent' Automakers – AMC to Willys 1945 to 1960 (Mort)
American Station Wagons – The Golden Era 1950-1975 (Mort)
American Trucks of the 1950s (Mort)
American Trucks of the 1960s (Mort)
American Woodies 1928-1953 (Mort)
Anglo-American Cars from the 1930s to the 1970s (Mort)
Austerity Motoring (Bobbitt)
Austins, The last real (Peck)
Brighton National Speed Trials (Gardiner)
British and European Trucks of the 1970s (Peck)
British Drag Racing – The early years (Pettitt)
British Lorries of the 1950s (Bobbitt)
British Lorries of the 1960s (Bobbitt)
British Touring Car Racing (Collins)
British Police Cars (Walker)
British Woodies (Peck)
Buick Riviera (Mort)
Café Racer Phenomenon, The (Walker)
Chevrolet 1/2-ton C/K-Series Pickup Trucks 1973-1987 (Mort)
Don Hayter's MGB Story – The birth of the MGB in MG's Abingdon Design & Development Office (Hayter)
Drag Bike Racing in Britain – From the mid '60s to the mid '80s (Lee)
Dune Buggy Phenomenon, The (Hale)
Dune Buggy Phenomenon Volume 2, The (Hale)
Endurance Racing at Silverstone in the 1970s & 1980s (Parker)
Hot Rod & Stock Car Racing in Britain in the 1980s (Neil)
Mercedes-Benz Trucks (Peck)
MG's Abingdon Factory (Moylan)
Motor Racing at Brands Hatch in the Seventies (Parker)
Motor Racing at Brands Hatch in the Eighties (Parker)
Motor Racing at Crystal Palace (Collins)
Motor Racing at Goodwood in the Sixties (Gardiner)
Motor Racing at Nassau in the 1950s & 1960s (O'Neil)
Motor Racing at Oulton Park in the 1960s (McFadyen)
Motor Racing at Oulton Park in the 1970s (McFadyen)
Motor Racing at Thruxton in the 1970s (Grant-Braham)
Motor Racing at Thruxton in the 1980s (Grant-Braham)
Superprix – The Story of Birmingham Motor Race (Page & Collins)
Three Wheelers (Bobbitt)

First published in May 2008, reprinted April 2020 by Veloce Publishing Limited, 33 Trinity Street, Dorchester DT1 1TT, England. Fax 01305 268864/e-mail info@veloce.co.uk/web www.veloce.co.uk or www.velocebooks.com.
ISBN: 1-845841-69-0/UPC: 6-36847-04169-4

© Colin Peck and Veloce Publishing 2008 & 2020. All rights reserved. With the exception of quoting brief passages for the purpose of review, no part of this publication may be recorded, reproduced or transmitted by any means, including photocopying, without the written permission of Veloce Publishing Ltd. Throughout this book logos, model names and designations, etc, have been used for the purposes of identification, illustration and decoration. Such names are the property of the trademark holder as this is not an official publication.
Readers with ideas for automotive books, or books on other transport or related hobby subjects, are invited to write to the editorial director of Veloce Publishing at the above address.
British Library Cataloguing in Publication Data - A catalogue record for this book is available from the British Library. Typesetting, design and page make-up all by Veloce Publishing Ltd on Apple Mac. Printed and bound by CPI Group (UK) Ltd, Croydon, CR0 4YY.

Contents

Foreword & acknowledgements 4

Introduction 5

Woodies at war 23

The chassis makers.. 37

The body builders .. .. .56

Beginning of the end 79

Restoring for tomorrow 85

Index. 95

Foreword & acknowledgements

Foreword

Wooden-bodied shooting brakes, station wagons and estate cars, collectively known as Woodies, were the original SUVs (sport utility vehicles). Whilst initially created for a specific purpose, their versatility, adaptability and load-carrying abilities meant that they quickly found favour with British buyers from all walks of life.

In their heyday, Woodies were built on virtually every make of car and light commercial chassis, and could be seen on every road in Britain. Sadly, in the 21st century, they are a rarity, due mostly to the fact that their wooden bodies were not built to last – and most didn't! Thousands were built by hundreds of different coachbuilders, both large and small, and, given the passage of time, it may never be possible to record all of their details with accuracy. This book isn't intended to be a definitive history, but just scratches the surface (pun intended) of these wooden wonders.

Colin Peck
Chairman, Woodie Car Club

Acknowledgements

John Blackman, Neill Bruce; John Colley; Archie Templeton-Dick; David Grounds; David Hardacre; David Hayward; Chris Moseley; ATT Papworth, Papworth Archives Project, Mike Parry, Peter Pattle, Pete Povey, Barrie Price, David Riley; Peter Sanders.

Introduction

This 1931 Rolls-Royce Phantom Safari wagon is a massive machine built to transport hunting parties.

This 1928 Rolls-Royce 20HP originally sported a Weymann saloon body, but was rebodied with Brakenvan bodywork to give the chassis an extra lease of life.

Over time, many have forgotten that the origin of the British-built, wooden-bodied shooting brake, estate car and station wagon, generically known as Woodies, is actually as obvious as their names imply.

These wood-framed, purpose-built vehicles were usually constructed in small production runs, built at a time when most major motor manufacturers had nothing in their product range between a family saloon and a light van. Woodies filled a gap, and were also built at a time when coachbuilding firms could be found in every virtually town in Britain, appearing on British roads when only the privileged could afford a motor car.

The first shooting brakes were intended, as the name implies, to carry shooting parties around private estates and game reserves. Early forerunners of the sport utility vehicle had a Rolls-Royce chassis, and many examples were built during the 1920s and 30s. Some were bodied from new as a shooting brake, whilst others began life as saloons, coupés or limousines, and were later rebodied as shooting brakes to give the chassis a second lease of life.

By the 1930s, the shooting brake had adopted a more general purpose role, and the term 'estate car' was coined to describe a vehicle that could still be used to carry shooting parties, yet, at the same time, be perfectly suitable for ferrying guests and their luggage to and from railway stations; groceries from the local village, or whisking the children off to boarding school. In essence, a true utility vehicle.

Historically, the two biggest markets for Woodies were the US and the UK. Whilst US Woodies can trace

This 1930 Rolls-Royce 20/25HP began life as an open tourer, and, apparently, was once owned by famous British composer, Benjamin Britten. It was converted to a shooting brake in the 1950s by Nash of Southampton.

their roots back to the open-sided depot Hacks and, latterly, station wagons used by resort hotels to collect guests and their luggage from railway stations, British shooting brakes were built originally for conveying wealthy land owners and their guests around private estates.

1935 Lanchester 10 with bodywork by Mulliner of Birmingham.

Some of the earliest Woodies were manufactured by Ford, such as this Canadian-built 1929 Model A.

British Woodies from the 1920s to the 1950s

Birth of the utility vehicle

During the 1930s cheap, mass-produced Ford V8 Woodies were imported to the UK from Canada, and set the scene for the utility or dual-purpose vehicle that was part car, part van – and even part bus. Whereas previously it was the norm to send large amounts of luggage by rail (as the average family car was rarely constructed to carry passengers and more than one small suitcase), the utility vehicle seemed to provide the perfect solution.

By the late 1930s, most British chassis manufacturers were acknowledging this new market sector by supplying chassis to specialist coachbuilders, and it was not unusual for humble Fords, Austins and Morrises to end up as utility estate cars. While the term 'shooting brake' had become generic by this time, many Woodies were built strictly as utility vehicles.

This 1932 Alvis 12/50 began life as a saloon before acquiring a second-hand Woodie body from an Alvis Silver Eagle.

Models such as the Brakenvan, Utilicon and Utilibrake had a much more workaday purpose, and their ability to carry both passengers and goods gave them a wider public appeal.

It must also be remembered that shooting brakes and utility brakes were legally classified as commercial vehicles, and therefore restricted to a maximum speed of 30mph (48kph) on British roads! A contemporary road test in *The Autocar* magazine, of the then new 1937 Ford V8 Utility Car speaks volumes about passenger comfort, luggage carrying capacity, and the vehicle's ability to gobble up mile after mile with ease, at an effortless

Alvis Silver Eagle shooting brake.

This 1932 Austin 10 began life as a four-door saloon before being converted to a utility by persons unknown.

This advert for the 'Studex' is typical of the 1930s when wood-framed bodywork usually lasted a few years only and a quality-built chassis often acquired several bodies during its serviceable life. Dex Garages of Newcastle-on-Tyne hit on the idea of converting second-hand Studebaker chassis into shooting brakes that had: "A built-in gun locker and full equipment, making it ideal for the sportsman and general estates and farm work."

1932 Lea-Francis 'Ace of Spades' Woodie.

British Woodies from the 1920s to the 1950s

cruising speed of 60mph (96kph). (The same report also mentions the tester's worry about being stopped by every village policeman he passed for exceeding the 30mph speed limit for light commercials.)

While Woodies followed a fairly natural and progressive evolution during the 1930s, the outbreak of WWII in Europe during 1939 resulted in tough new motoring laws in Britain, which were to change the course of Woodie history. The first of these measures was the introduction of petrol rationing, so that more fuel could be diverted to the war effort.

The initial allowance for private motoring equated – depending on model of car – to enough fuel to cover between 100 and 200 miles a month. Commercial vehicles, on the other hand, got a bigger allowance, which made ownership of a shooting brake (legally classified as a commercial vehicle) an even more attractive proposition.

Tax exemption for Woodies

By July 1940, the British government had commandeered stocks of all new cars and summarily banned their purchase by private individuals, except under special circumstances. By October that year, production of private cars had ceased altogether, so that car makers could give their undivided attention to the production of heavy equipment for the war effort.

At the same time, the British government introduced a new form of retail taxation known as purchase tax. This was levied at 33 per cent on the price of all new cars (providing, of course, you could lay your hands on one), but not on commercial vehicles – another major plus point for owning a Woodie.

In the years that followed a large number of structurally sound saloon cars – those not already

This 1937 Wolseley 25 Woodie is a very imposing car. It was originally bodied in Scotland, then rebuilt by the son of the original coachbuilder in the 1990s.

requisitioned by the War Department – were driven, or most likely pushed, into the workshops of local coachbuilders across the UK, where the rear half of the body was cut off and replaced with more appropriate commercial bodywork. Many were converted to wooden-bodied utilities as, with metal supplies diverted to the war effort, conversion to ash-framed bodywork was a simple screw and glue job.

Some of these conversions were crude, whilst others were on a par with the work of the best coachbuilders. Many of the larger-engined, gas-guzzling 6 cylinder and 8 cylinder North American cars – such as Buicks, Chryslers, Hudsons, Packards, Plymouths and Studebakers – that were so popular on pre-war British roads, were converted in this way.

Large cars required by the War Department were

Introduction

This 1½-litre 1939 MG VA was originally an open sports car, but was converted during World War II to a utility by University Motors for its owner, Major A T G Gardner.

During WWII a number of large-engined, North American-built saloons were converted to Woodies in order to make better use of available vehicles, as well as ensuring a commercial vehicle petrol ration. This Packard sports wartime white bumpers and running board edges, but is devoid of headlight covers, so the photo may have been taken after hostilities ended.

Commer made a brief foray into the utility market in the mid to late 1930s. This version has bodywork by Kevill Davies and was followed in 1939 by the launch of the 8cwt Commer 'Tender'. (Courtesy C K Bowers)

usually turned into ambulances, fire tenders, mobile canteens, vans, and even light trucks. Once hostilities ceased, and these service vehicles were no longer needed to perform the same role, they became prime candidates for conversion to Woodies. In fact, many of the nation's small coachbuilding firms thrived in the early post-war years by converting military surplus vehicles to Woodies, which were eagerly snapped up by a public starved of 'new' vehicles for more than five years.

Export or die

A number of circumstances in post-war Britain combined to create a unique situation in which Woodie production soared to new heights, making the period between 1946-54 the golden years of the shooting brake. The first post-war government budget occurred in 1945 and retained the 33 per cent purchase tax (PT) on private cars, whilst commercials and shooting brake derivatives remained exempt. This, in addition to a number of other factors, combined to make Woodies an extremely popular mode of transport during this time.

Within a month of the end of war in Europe, the British government began easing restrictions on the motor industry so that production of cars could begin again. However, while the Board of Trade and Ministry of Supply sanctioned 200,000 cars in total to be built by the entire British motor industry during the following twelve months, it also decreed that 50 per cent would

The 'official' Commer utility was almost identical to the Kevill Davies-bodied cars, with the exception of some minor styling changes.

British Woodies from the 1920s to the 1950s

This unique 1949 Fordson was owned by the Ford Motor Company in the UK from 1949 until 2005, and it is thought that its lines reflect those of 1935-39 North American Woodies.

Introduction

This 1951 Ford Pilot V8 Woodie is rumoured to have begun life as a bread van before being converted to a passenger carrier.

Introduction

Left: This 1948 Standard 14 is believed to be a rare factory-built car.

have to be exported to help pay off the huge war debts that Britain had incurred.

This export figure was subsequently increased to 75 per cent which the government was able to enforce as it controlled the supply of steel that was rationed to car manufacturers. During this period the term 'export or die' was the watchword, and manufacturers became adapt at conserving those vital steel supplies.

In Britain there was a huge market for new cars of any size or shape, though most buyers would have to wait years to take delivery after placing an order. Despite the steel shortages, there was a plentiful supply of wood and no restrictions on the supply of aluminium, so some owners found it possible to jump the queue by purchasing a car chassis and having it bodied by a local

Lea-Francis was one of the first companies to exploit the tax loophole of supplying Woodie vans, which could later have the upper side wooden panels replaced with windows, and a rear seat installed to turn them into a passenger vehicle.

British Woodies from the 1920s to the 1950s

The production line at Papworth Industries, where 500 Austin 16 Countryman estate cars were bodied for Austin.

coachbuilder. In fact, many specialised manufacturers, such as Alvis and Lea-Francis, found that chassis production often outstripped body supply.

More significantly, there were no restrictions on the supply of light commercial chassis cabs, which not only required less steel to build, but were designed to help Britain rebuild itself after the war, and so were readily available. All of these factors combined to make the Woodie one of the most popular vehicles during the tough post-war years.

Britain already had a rich heritage of small commercial coachbuilders, whose expertise in building wood-framed van, truck and bus bodywork gave them an edge during the early post-war years when metal was in short supply. They quickly found that wooden-bodied, car-sized vehicles were eagerly snapped up by the car-starved public, and supplies of new chassis could also be augmented with large numbers of light commercial chassis, and even Jeeps and other ex-military chassis found at various war surplus sales.

Many coachbuilders bodied vehicles in their own name, while some leading car dealers had contracts with local coachbuilders, whose work usually went unacknowledged. Some car makers also took to branding their factory-approved estate cars as 'utility' models in advertising and literature, as if to reaffirm their tax-free status. However, the quality of workmanship – and particularly the materials used – in the construction of some Woodies produced to exploit this tax loophole was often suspect. Some utility vehicles were built as cheaply as possible; often, opening rear side doors were omitted or sealed shut, and rear doors fitted instead of split tailgates.

Lea-Francis took the 'utility' theme a stage further and built Woodie vans, many of which omitted rear seats and side windows completely. These vans could be, and frequently were, upgraded to estate car specification.

Factory-approved Woodies

Austin was one of the first manufacturers to launch its own factory-approved Woodie, after securing a deal with Papworth Industries in Cambridgeshire for the construction of 250 Austin 16 shooting brakes. While Alvis didn't offer its own 'approved' Woodie, Lea-Francis did. After having a number of 14HP chassis bodied by a variety of body builderss, the Coventry car maker did a deal with AP Aircraft of Coventry to build its regular saloon bodies, as well as a large number of utility shooting brakes. Records show that more than 1000 Lea-Francis utility vehicles were constructed between 1945-54.

The car-derived Austin A70 Hampshire pickup chassis cab proved particularly popular during this period, and a number of body builderss emulated the lines of the official A70 Countryman BW3 that Papworth Industries built for Austin Motors, after production of the Austin16 had ended.

While approximately 95 per cent of BW3s went for export, clones were built up and down the country, and London-based Austin dealer, Cart Mart, even acquired a batch of 200 A70 chassis cabs which it sent to Papworth for bodying as shooting brakes. These fulfilled a wide variety of roles, and were used as TV outside broadcast units and support tenders for racing car teams, as well as the more traditional use of carrying hotel guests and their luggage to and from railway stations and ports.

In post-war years, Woodies became increasingly expensive to build, and the use of external wood

British Woodies from the 1920s to the 1950s

Cars with ash-framed bodywork often make great candidates for rebuilding into a Woodie, such as this Riley RM 1½-litre conversion.

While post-war Daimlers were, sadly, not a popular chassis choice for shooting brake bodies, this superb example was created on a DB18. (Courtesy Neill Bruce)

framing and panels required a high level of bodywork maintenance by owners in order to prevent the body losing its structural integrity. So, while there was a distinct niche market for the utility car, the wooden-bodied shooting brake was never a high volume seller.

After decades of building vehicles with separate chassis and bodies, in the early 50s the British motor industry moved more and more to the mass-production of unitary construction cars, and this, more than anything else, finally killed off the coachbuilt Woodie. With sales

British Woodies from the 1920s to the 1950s

Whitacres of Stoke-on-Trent built this unusual Austin A40-based Woodie. As it was a van, the owner did not have to pay purchase tax. The upper side wooden panels could later be replaced with glass, converting the van to a passenger-carrying vehicle.

already low, introduction of purchase tax on commercial vehicles in April 1950 saw Woodie sales fall even further.

Both Alvis and Lea-Francis were hard hit, yet Austin soldiered on until 1954 when the last separate chassis A70 Countryman rolled off the Papworth production line. Although the coachbuilt Woodie's era ended at this time, Morris Motors had introduced the Oxford MO Traveller in June 1952, followed a year later by the mass-produced Minor Traveller – a car that was to make Woodies available to the masses ... but that's another story ...

Visit Veloce on the web: www.veloce.co.uk
Information on all books • New book news • Special offers • Gift vouchers

Woodies at war

One of the most often overlooked aspects of the history of the shooting brake in Britain is the role it played supporting Allied forces during World War II, both on the home front and in a number of overseas campaigns. Britain had begun preparing for hostilities as soon as the war clouds darkened over Europe in the late 1930s, and, as new vehicles were ordered for use by the armed forces, so ended the founding chapter in the role of the shooting brake.

No longer used primarily to service the needs of the landed gentry, these wooden-bodied vehicles now adopted a general purpose utility role, to which they were ideally suited. Production records are sketchy in some areas, but the main manufacturers of these wartime Woodies used by British forces were Ford, Humber, and Standard. A few General Motors-based Woodies were photographed in action in North Africa and the Middle East, but no records have yet been found on models and numbers produced.

Humber began military Super Snipe MkII production in the summer of 1939, with body styles ranging from staff car, open tourer, light truck, and the utility car. It is believed that a total of 1500 four-door utility bodies were constructed by the Rootes Group's specialist coachbuilder, Thrupp & Maberley, sporting mesh grilles instead of chrome and the same 900x13

continued page 29

Super Snipe MkII production ranged from staff car to open tourer, light truck, and the utility car. A small number of two-door variants, such as this one, were produced primarily for use by the RAF.

Standard produced a number of 12HP 'Tilly' pickups for the War Department, some of which were used by the RAF. An unknown number were bodied as utilities, and it is believed that some may have been used on the home front as non-stretcher case ambulances. The history of this rare survivor is unknown. (Courtesy Rolland Playford)

Woodies at war

While it is not known how many Humber utilities were lost to enemy action, or, indeed, left behind on the beaches at Dunkirk, this particular example sustained major frontal damage as a result of a collision with a larger vehicle.
(Courtesy Imperial War Museum, reference O1114)

This Humber utility undergoes some maintenance checks in the motor pool. (Courtesy www.stilltime.net)

This photo, taken in 1940 near Douai in France, shows officers of the Cheshire Regiment at the 'Colonel's morning conference.'
(Courtesy Imperial War Museum, reference F3166)

Many Humber utilities never saw front line service, like this example, photographed in July 1940, in support of the army laundry service. (Courtesy www.stilltime.net)

wheels and tyres as Canadian-built Fords. A small number of two-door variants were also produced and used primarily by the Royal Air Force.

The Dunkirk evacuation of 1941 played a big part in shaping the role that Ford of Canada was to play in the supply of utility-bodied vehicles for the British army. With 84,000 allied vehicles left behind in France and on Dunkirk's beaches, and the Luftwaffe mounting round-the-clock attacks against British industry, British forces were running short of resources. A large number of Humber utility wagons were lost at Dunkirk and, as the design was ageing fast, most of those that survived were removed from frontline service, instead, mostly taking up support roles in the UK.

The success of the Canadian-built 30HP Ford V8 utility wagon introduced in 1937 had shown the way forward, and a small number, fitted with huge, 900x13 tyres for off-road use, were ordered by the British army. These were followed in 1938 by the model 81A, and bigger orders for the 1939 model.

So, while the industrial might of the US was in the early stages of gearing up for war, much of Britain's requirement for trucks and staff cars was destined to be met by the Canadians. The need for a heavy utility car was fulfilled by variants of the standard North American 1941 station wagon as a result of contracts – termed 'Supply Mechanical' – from the British War Office.

The heaviest version was the C11ADF, Canadian-assembled 1941 model Woodie with an 85bHP motor. It was specified with a heavy duty rear axle, large 900x13 sand tyres, and right-hand-drive. Militarised versions of the 1941 (C11AS) and 1942 (C21AS) station wagons with standard suspension neatly filled the gap and did a superb job, although they were often known to overheat

British Woodies from the 1920s to the 1950s

Woodies at war

This Canadian-built 1941 Ford C11ADF was one of many such vehicles used by British forces across North Africa. It was fairly common for accident-damaged Woodies to have their roofs removed in this way.
(Courtesy Imperial War Museum, reference E23761)

This Ford Woodie was assigned to the artillery regiment, and is seen here giving the signal for one complete battery to advance in desert formation.
(Courtesy Imperial War Museum, reference E9116)

British Woodies from the 1920s to the 1950s

The Canadian-built Ford C11AS was a militarised version of the civilian 1941 Ford Woodie that was supplied to the British Army during World War II.

Woodies at war

in convoy situations; many period photographs show extra air vents, air scoops and louvres cut into bonnets to try and overcome this problem.

Many of these Fords were used in various North African campaigns. On arrival at the battle front, many had hatches crudely cut into the roof above

In 1942, the SAS used a cut down Ford C11ADF – known as the 'Blitz Buggy' – in a number of clandestine operations against German and Italian positions in North Africa. The vehicle was ultimately destroyed in 1942 by gunfire from an Italian aircraft, but has been lovingly recreated by military historian, Peter Sanders. (Courtesy John Blackman)

British Woodies from the 1920s to the 1950s

the front passenger, and some even had the top removed completely and the doors bolted shut. These modifications were mostly for aircraft observation purposes, although sometimes the bodywork modifications were a direct result of enemy action.

While the exact number of C11ADFs produced is uncertain, the first contract 'Supply Mechanical number 2027' was placed during the summer of 1941, and was for a total of 498 vehicles, of which at least 442 were delivered. The rest, perhaps, were lost at sea during a perilous North Atlantic crossing.

The second contract, number 2044, dated 4th August 1941, was for 998 station wagons, all of which seemed to have been delivered by August 1943. Ultimately, the Ford C11ADF was by far the most popular passenger transport in North Africa campaigns. After the war, those that survived and made it back to British shores were demobbed in around 1947, and immediately pressed into civilian use by the car-starved population.

The Standard Motor Company also played a small part in supplying Woodies to the War Department; 'square cut' vehicles which were based on Standard 12 running gear, with bodies by Remploy. It is doubtful if any saw active service and were most likely used in support

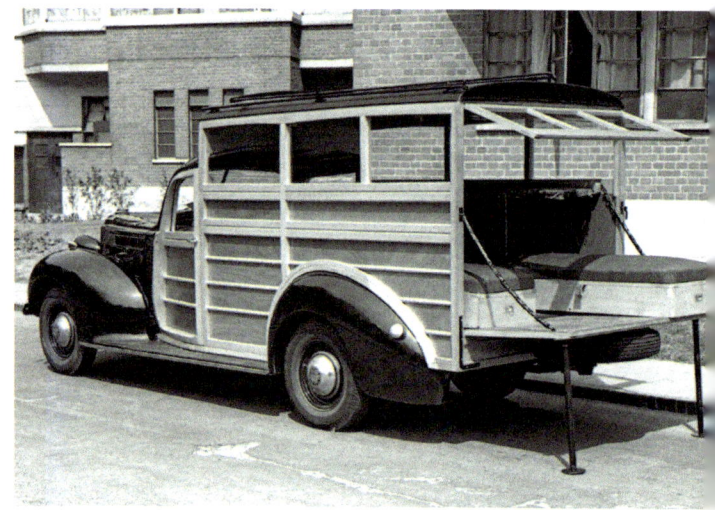

This cut down Packard saloon car has been turned into a wooden-bodied medical car with two slide out beds. (Courtesy www.stilltime.net)

This 1934 Bentley 3½-litre originally had Park Ward open tourer bodywork, before its owner donated it to the RAF Benevolent Fund at the outbreak of World War II. Who constructed the 'new' bodywork is not known, as the car was rediscovered in the 1970s with its current body. It is most likely that it was converted to a load-carrying Woodie during the war so that the commercial vehicle ration of petrol could be obtained.

Woodies at war

roles, such as a non-stretcher case ambulance – a role to which Woodies were ideally suited.

In addition to the Woodies that were ordered direct from chassis manufacturers, a great many large British and American saloon cars were converted to wartime utilities, a number specifically constructed to fulfil the role of non-stretcher case ambulances.

This Bentley was converted to an RAF tender by Wallis & Co. It is seen here in 1941 at an unknown industrial location. (Courtesy www.stilltime.net)

Kidd Brothers of Clacton built a number of Woodies on stretched war surplus Jeep chassis.

This 1935 Rolls-Royce 20/25 was delivered new in Rhodesia as a 'hunting car,' and was then seized by the Germans during World War II and used as a staff car. After the war it was purchased by William Wrigley, of Wrigley's Chewing Gum fame, and used as a shooting brake on his private reserve on Catalina Island. It has now been returned to the UK where it is, once again, being used as a shooting brake on a private game reserve.

British Woodies from the 1920s to the 1950s

Willenhall Coachcraft built between 80 and 90 Woodies on war surplus Jeeps for use on game reserves and country estates.

Despite its humble Jeep chassis, Willenhall Coachcraft incorporated some interesting curves and design features in its wooden bodywork.

The chassis makers

While just about every conceivable make of British car and light commercial chassis received wooden shooting brake bodywork at some stage, most Woodies were built in small, sometimes very small, batches by specialist workshops or commercial body builderss who had honed their skills constructing van, truck, and bus bodies. Most of these companies, often because they were working as a sub-contractor to a garage or car dealer, were never allowed to put their name to the bodywork, with the result that there are many Woodies in existence in Britain today for which the body builder is unknown.

Some of the most popular types of post-war Woodies in Britain were built on Alvis, Austin, Ford, and Lea-Francis chassis. However, whereas both Austin and Lea-Francis sold factory-approved vehicles, those available on Alvis and Ford chassis were constructed by numerous independent coachbuilding firms.

Allard

Victory in the 1952 Monte Carlo Rally must have made Allard a familiar name in many markets in which sports cars were not of great interest but where fast, roadworthy and large-load capacity cars were required. So Allard saloon and convertible models were supplemented in spring that year by the Safari – a six seater, two-door estate car version of the P2 saloon, with the lusty sidevalve Ford V8 motor as the standard power option. The model was, supposedly, only available for export, and was discontinued in 1955 after only 10 had been built.

Alvis

Alvis was a popular choice of chassis during the 1930s, and many shabby saloons got a second lease of life with a wooden utility body. The post-war TA14 proved exceedingly popular as a shooting brake, although there was no official Alvis version. Records show that 145 chassis were supplied to known coachbuilders, whilst a further 120 are listed as being delivered as utilities – coachbuilder unknown.

Just ten of Sydney Allard's P2-derived Safari estate cars were built. most destined for export. Just two are known to be UK-based, and this is the only example powered by the lusty Ford sidevalve, 3.6-litre V8, as used in the Ford Pilot. As if to prove that the big Allard is no slouch, it is seen here at a Brands Hatch track day.

The attractive lines of this Wyatt-bodied Alvis TA14 show distinct US influences, particularly at the rear.

The chassis makers

In addition, Alvis records show a further 465 TA 14 chassis listed as body type unknown, so it's possible that many of these also ended up with shooting brake bodies.

Most of the new chassis that were delivered to coachbuilders were shipped complete with front bulkhead, dashboard, and front seats – which explains why so many ended up with luxurious leather front seats and utilitarian rear seats. Most numerically significant were the cars bodied by Gaze Limited, believed to have been based in Kingston-upon-Thames, and also responsible for many Lea-Francis Woodies. However, Gaze is not thought to have sold cars under its own name, and was sub-contracted by Alvis dealerships such as Brooklands of Bond Street, Vincents of Reading, and Reliance Garage of Norwich. All these companies attached their own nameplates to the bodywork, helping to create the myth that dealers had bodied the cars themselves.

The second most numerous Alvis coachbuilder was the Jones company. As with Gaze, little is known about this company, although records show that it also bodied a number of Rolls-Royces. At the height of TA14 popularity, companies such as Abbotts of Farnham, AC Cars, Barnards, Black & White, Caffyns, and even Carmichael, produced Alvis Woodies.

In most cases, either a car or an old photo survives to record what each Woodie design looked like, with one exception: it seems that quite a few Alvis utilities are listed as being bodied by High Elms, but these are a mystery in Alvis circles as there are no photos or records of any survivors.

This unique 'aeroback' two-door Woodie saloon was once owned by MP Jack Straw.

British Woodies from the 1920s to the 1950s

Austin

Whilst Austin can't lay claim to building the first or last Woodies in the UK, few realise that Austin was actually one of the most prolific builders of wooden-bodied estate cars during the Woodie's heyday.

Despite not previously having offered a full-scale production utility, Austin was keen to add a shooting brake to its vehicle line-up in the immediate post-war period, as this was a great way to help achieve the government export quota, and Woodies required much less steel in their construction.

History was in the making when Frank Jordon – former head coachbuilder for the London General Omnibus Company, and later head of the carpentry workshops at Papworth Industries in Cambridgeshire – turned up at Austin's Longbridge works. Frank had heard that Austin was looking for a company to build shooting brake bodies on the Austin 16 chassis, so he went to Longbridge, knocked on the right door, and walked away with an order to build 250 Woodies.

The fact that Papworth Industries built the 250 Woodies faster than expected, and to a higher than anticipated quality, so impressed the bean counters at Longbridge that they ordered 250 more. These 500 Austin 16s were designated by Austin as BW1, and were the first in a major Woodie-building programme that was to continue until 1954. It seems likely that the Countryman name was born with the Austin 16 Woodie, as, whilst an early brochure describes these vehicles as shooting brakes, the most common version of the same brochure calls them Countryman.

Austin was so pleased with the quality of the Countryman vehicles bodied by Papworth Industries that, when the Austin 16 was replaced by the post-war-designed A70 Hampshire, orders for more than 900 Countryman Woodies, designated BW3, were placed. These were all based on the Austin BS2 Hampshire A70 saloon chassis and body, so retained the car's 16 inch wheels, high ratio differential, and steel floor of the saloon body.

The car-derived Austin A70 Hampshire pickup chassis cab also proved particularly popular during this time, and a number of body builders emulated the design of the A70 Countryman BW3. While almost 90 per cent of BW3s went for export, London-based Austin dealer, Car Mart, sent 200 A70 pickup chassis cabs to Papworth Industries to be bodied as shooting brakes, and these were ultimately used as everything from TV outside broadcast units to support vehicles for motor racing teams, as well as in the traditional role of carrying hotel guests and their luggage to and from railway stations and ports.

The A70 Hampshire was replaced by the A70 Hereford at the end of 1950, and, within a few months, the A70 Hereford BW4 Countryman Woodie had been designed and was being built at Papworth. The BW4 went on to become the most popular of all Austin Woodies, with more than 1500 built before the A70 went

Left: Papworth Industries bodied 500 Austin 16 Countryman models for Austin between 1947 and 1949.

More than 900 of these sleek A70 Hampshire Countryman estates were built by Papworth Industries for Austin, yet only seven are believed to survive worldwide. At the time of writing, this is the only example thought to be roadworthy.

British Woodies from the 1920s to the 1950s

out of production at the end of 1954. It was replaced by the unitary construction Austin A90 Westminster, though, sadly, it was not possible to build a Westminster Woodie.

Steel shortages eased in the early 1950s. Wood-framed bodies had grown costly to build, were very labour-intensive to maintain, and, in many cases were not able to withstand the harsh treatment they received on the poor road conditions of many export markets. However, the demise of the separate chassis also heralded the end of the Woodie; Austin never built it again.

Ford

Ford entered the utility car market in the UK during the mid 1930s by supplying V8-powered station wagons that were assembled at Ford's Windsor, Ontario plant in Canada. The wooden bodies were constructed at Ford's bodywork facility at Iron Mountain in Michigan, USA, and shipped to Canada for assembly on V8 chassis.

The cars were mostly complete when they arrived in the UK, receiving final finishing at the Ford plant in Dagenham, where some trim items and the UK specification wiring loom were fitted. By the late 1930s, UK-built sidevalve V8 engines were also being installed. These were the only 'official' Ford Woodies sold in the UK, as, although a large number of 10HP Ford car, and even Fordson van chassis, were bodied by UK coachbuilders during the 1930s, Ford never offered a factory-built small Woodie.

While Ford had helped establish the utility car market in the UK during the 1930s, it didn't re-enter that market after the cessation of hostilities at the end of WWII, though did supply a number of E71C Pilot

Ford was the only North American-based manufacturer to bring fully-assembled Woodies into the UK, like this 1935 Canadian-built V8 'Utility Car.' (Courtesy C K Bowers)

commercial chassis to dealers and individuals, who had them bodied as estate cars. A number survive today, and yet it is rare to find two that look the same, such was the diversity of building styles and techniques employed in their construction.

Lea-Francis

Lea-Francis tooled up for the production of its first post-war model, the 14HP four-door saloon, in 1945. The new car was essentially a modified version of the 12.9HP saloon, produced in limited numbers between 1938 and 1940, and mostly bodied by Avon Bodies of Warwick. The body was constructed by a local Coventry sheet

The chassis makers

Canadian-built 1936 Ford V8 utility.

The chassis makers

The bodywork of this 1937 22HP Ford V8 has the distinctive Brakenvan styling, and may have been built under franchise by Kevill Davies and March. (Courtesy C K Bowers)

metal factory, A P Aircraft (APA), from a combination of steel and aluminium, and formed the backbone of Lea-Francis production until the company ceased volume manufacture in 1954.

The Coventry-based company was also one of the first to see the potential of the wooden-bodied utility in post-war Britain, and, during 1946, commissioned Riverlee Bodies of Birmingham to construct its first ever Woodie van.

Lea-Francis then commissioned the Southern Caravan Company of Yapton, near Chichester, to build

A road test of the 1937 Ford series 78 V8 Utility Car by *The Autocar* magazine had the tester extolling the virtues of 60mph (96kph) cruising, though worried about breaking the 30mph (48kph) speed limit imposed on commercial vehicles.

Hollers of Bristol bodied this 1950 Ford Pilot V8.

A variation on the Ford Pilot theme by an unknown body builder.

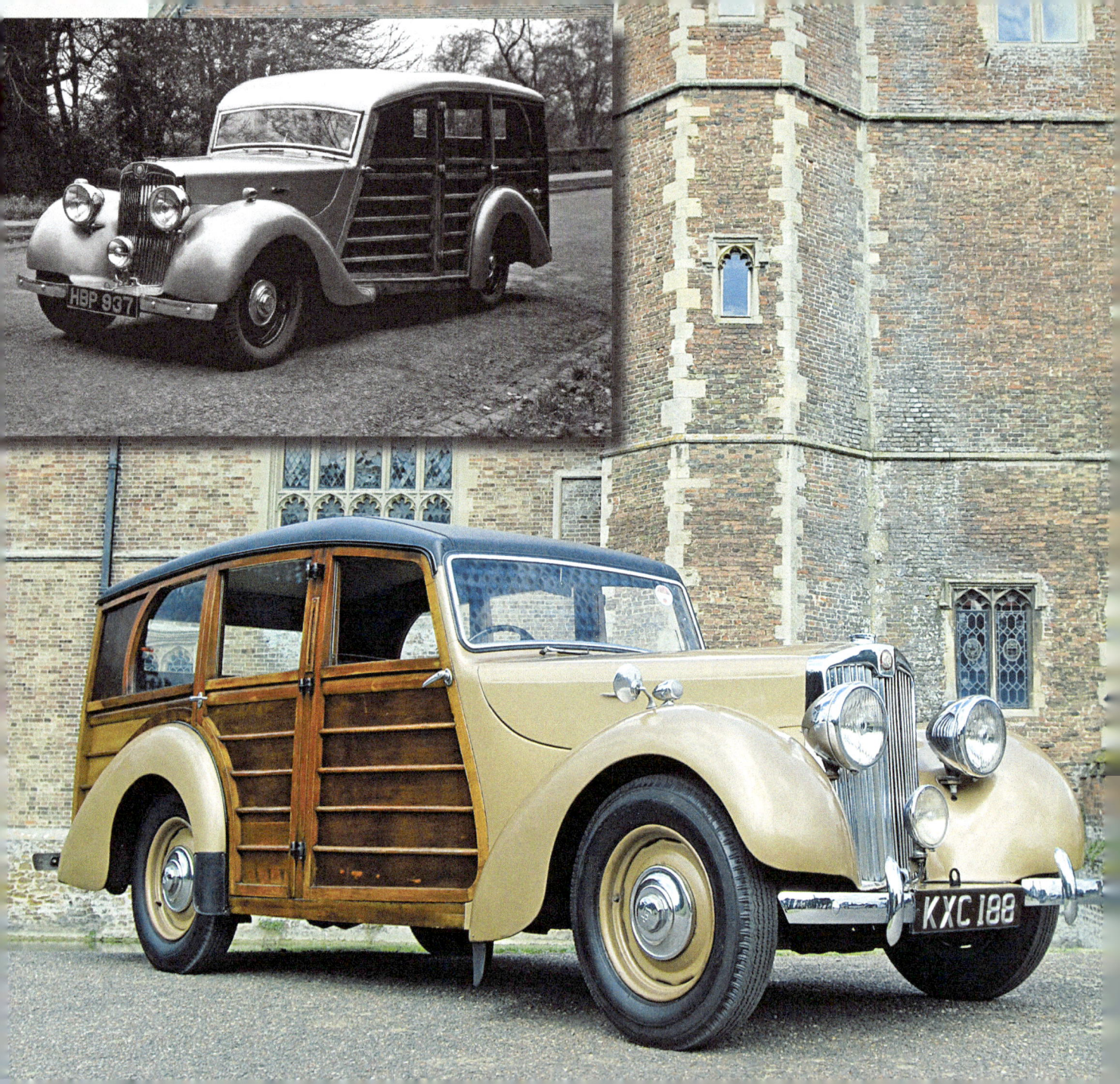

The chassis makers

Inset, left: 1946 Lea-Francis Utility with bodywork by the Yapton Caravan Company.

Left: 1950 Lea-Francis with in-house utility bodywork by APA.

estate cars; by the end of 1946, 74 Woodies had been built by a variety of coachbuilders, including Southern Caravans.

As Woodies were designated commercial vehicles (thus avoiding the payment of purchase tax on the list price of new cars), the new Lea-Francis estate car was described as a 'utility model' in the company's literature, and a further 44 were built at Yapton during 1947. Records also show that at least 80 chassis were supplied to individual coachbuilders that year – most ending up as Woodies – although one or two were actually built as ice cream vans.

A number of coachbuilders found that the Lea-Francis 14HP chassis was absolutely perfect as the basis of a shooting brake, with companies like Jensen Motors, Gaze, and Frank Grounds building bodies for both Lea-Francis and rival Alvis. While there are no accurate records of exactly who built Woodie bodies on Lea-Francis chassis, factory records do show that almost 500 'chassis only' units were supplied to builders of estate cars and vans during 1948/49. It was during this time that the contract to build the 'factory' Woodies went to APA – the company already building the saloon car bodies for Lea-Francis.

One of the most interesting aspects of Lea-Francis Woodie production was the range of vans it produced alongside the estate cars. In essence, these were utility cars without the rear seats and plywood panels where the side windows would normally be. They also had

Sadly, Lea-Francis ceased building cars in 1954, and the last two 14HP chassis received stylish Woodie bodies by Papworth Industries.

Left: 1951 Lea-Francis with APA bodywork.

This artist's impression was created by Papworth Industries for a more modern Lea-Francis Woodie state car. Unfortunately, Lea-Francis ceased trading before the sketch could be transformed into a complete vehicle.

British Woodies from the 1920s to the 1950s

rear doors as an alternative to tailgates, and, in many cases, side rear doors that could not be opened. Whilst they were cheaper to produce than the estate cars, they were still much more expensive than the mass-produced 'metal panelled' vans available from the likes of Austin, Bedford, Ford, and Morris.

In 1950, a Lea-Francis estate was an unlikely entrant in the Monte Carlo Rally, with an Isle of Man-registered vehicle starting from Glasgow and finishing in 103rd place without any trouble. The same year the company sold 123 utility estates and 67 vans. By now, however, the cars' pre-war styling was beginning to look a little dated; without the financial resources necessary to design a completely new car, Lea-Francis restyled the front of the car only – the headlamps were incorporated into the front wings – for 1951.

The 1951 season did see a slight upturn in sales, with 175 estates but just 2 vans sold. Prices for all models increased considerably for that year, which further contributed to a drop in sales.

Sadly, like so many car makers of the day that could not afford to build the stylish new models the public wanted, the writing was on the wall for Lea-Francis. Sales of estate cars suffered badly in 1952, with only four sold – the last of which went to Tasmania.

The Lea-Francis 14HP estate car continued, alongside the saloon, right up until production ceased in 1954 – curiously enough, the last two chassis built (10064 and 10066) were fitted with a handsome new estate car body by Papworth Industries, which was also building wooden bodies for the much more modern Austin A70 Hereford.

Whilst no precise figures exist, it is estimated that around 1000 Lea-Francis Woodie estate cars and vans were built between 1946 and 1955. Survival rate has

For the first two months of production, Morris MO Oxford Travellers had the early-type mazak chromed grille: this car has been restored to that specification.

The first 'Traveller's car' was the wood-framed Morris Oxford MO Traveller. It entered production in June 1952, four years after introduction of the Oxford MO saloon. It was followed just over a year later by a three-quarter scale version – the Morris Minor Traveller.

This superb atmospheric shot shows an MO Traveller being used as a 'radio car' to support the Nuffield Organisation's MO-hauled test rig containing a Morris Minor. One has to assume that the test route didn't contain any low bridges! (Courtesy www.stilltime.net)

The ubiquitous Morris Minor Traveller was launched at the October 1953 London Earl's Court motor show, and more than 250,000 were built before production finally ended in 1971. (Courtesy John Colley)

been poor, unfortunately, with just 30 estate cars and vans in running or restorable condition known to the Lea-Francis Owners Club. These figures compare very closely with the Lea-Francis' closest rival, the 14HP Alvis, also built in Coventry and clothed in saloon and estate car bodywork of similar design.

Morris

Whilst the coachbuilt Woodie was slowly, but surely, heading for oblivion, a new twist in the tale was provided by Morris Motors. In 1952, the company launched a wooden-framed estate car version of its popular unitary construction Morris MO Oxford sedan, which had been launched in 1948. Dubbed the Traveller, the new Morris was intended for a completely new market for Woodies: the travelling salesman, and those that needed to carry goods, passengers, and even livestock in the same vehicle.

It was the company's first foray into the dual-purpose market, and, remarkably, the MO Traveller was not based on the van/pickup chassis, but used a reinforced version of the saloon's mono-construction floorpan. Thus, the wood was a structural part of the car's assembly, which probably accounts for why few survive today. Construction of the timber-framed rear section was undertaken at the Morris Bodies factory in Coventry, where it was assembled with painted aluminium panel and full glazing, and then shipped, as a complete unit, by road to the main assembly lines in Cowley.

The logistical problem of marrying the wooden back section to the main cab and floor was overcome within a special area at Cowley called the 'loft.' This was located above the assembly lines, and it was here that the back sections were stored, prior to being lowered to the main assembly area, where, in a complicated operation, they were joined to the painted chassis cab.

Records show that 5500 MO Travellers were built between summer 1952 and spring 1954, and exported to a number of European countries as well as Canada, though it seems that the majority were shipped to Australia and summarily shaken to bits on Australia's outback roads!

Curiously, when Morris merged with rival Austin later in 1952 to form the British Motor Corporation, there must have been some interesting boardroom discussions about the various advantages and disadvantages of the large Austin A70 Countryman versus the medium-sized Morris Oxford Traveller. In the end, it was Morris that was destined to fly the Woodie flag into the future, though it was not the part-timbered Oxford series II or Isis Traveller that would conclude this emotive chapter of British motoring history, but the humble Morris Minor Traveller launched in 1953.

A prototype Minor Traveller had been built in 1951, but it wasn't until the BMC A-series ohv engine was installed that sales began to take off. It is estimated that a quarter of a million Morris Minor Travellers were built before production was finally halted in 1971, and one of its many claims to fame is that large numbers were sold to the British army in 1968, many of which were used in Germany.

While Ford in the UK made various attempts during the 1950s and 60s to revive the Woodie look on estate cars, the Minor remained true to ash-framed construction right to the very end, and can fairly and squarely lay claim to being the world's last production Woodie.

Visit Veloce on the web: www.veloce.co.uk
Information on all books • New book news • Special offers • Gift vouchers

The body builders

Exactly how many British coachbuilding firms constructed wooden-framed shooting brake bodies will probably never be known, but the number is certainly high. Most Woodies were not built by the companies associated with luxurious limousines or elegant coupés, but, instead, were constructed by small independent commercial coachbuilding firms that were adept at bodying vans, trucks, and buses. Many were even built by local village carpenters!

Numerous coachbuilding firms started out as cartage and haulage companies, progressing to building their own truck bodies and then expanding into a full-blown coachbuilding business. There was tremendous variety in both style and quality of build; the vehicle buyer, unfortunately, not always able to distinguish between bodywork that was well-constructed and that which was quite appalling.

Alvis was one of the chassis manufacturers which had entered the Woodie market by default. Due to problems it had experienced with body builders prior to World War II, Alvis had intended that only completed cars would leave the factory after the war. However, a shortage of new saloon bodies resulted in the company selling chassis cowls. The fact that a utility vehicle attracted no purchase tax meant that a Woodie could be put on the road for about £250 less than a factory-built saloon, an appealing proposition for buyers, many of whom made even greater savings by using a less reputable body builder.

Alvis insisted that the coachbuilder return the completed vehicle to the works for a safety inspection, before a guarantee could be validated. The Alvis tester of the day reports that most Woodies were well built, but some needed much remedial work before the guarantee could be issued.

Some coachbuilders built batches of cars for marque dealers such as Brooklands of Bond Street in London. While these vehicles were sold under the Brooklands name, in fact, most were constructed by Gaze Ltd of Kingston-upon-Thames. However, most of the smaller coachbuilders built vehicles which they sold themselves, and many were constructed to specific customer orders, which accounts for the great variance in design, style and construction, and a number of unique one-offs.

A good example of the problem facing a historian trying to research the subject today is that of

Whilst not considered a mainstream body builder, AC Cars did body two beautifully proportioned Alvis TA14s – this example still survives.

The only Invicta Black Prince Woodie ever built. Just 16 post-war Invictas were produced before the company folded, and Woodie bodywork was built on the last chassis to leave the factory. It seems a visiting truck driver was able to purchase the chassis on the very last day before the company closed, and took it to local bus builder, Associated Coachcraft of Sunderland, which produced this unique car. The car survives and currently has Jaguar XJ6 axles.

British Woodies from the 1920s to the 1950s

Lea-Francis, which records almost 500 chassis being supplied to more than 100 independent shooting brake coachbuilders. Sadly, most of the vehicles – together with details of the location of the coachbuilder concerned – have long since disappeared without trace.

Whilst not exhaustive, the following list details some of the more noteworthy coachbuilders:

Angel Motor Bodies

Angel Motor Bodies of Trafford Park, Manchester, specialised in giving pre-war cars a more modern look, and was responsible for contemporarily-styled wooden bodywork on Rovers, Armstrong Siddeleys, Jaguars, Bentley, Lagondas, Rileys, and Austins.

Bonallack

East London-based Bonallack was, perhaps, best known for building alloy truck cabs, bodies and trailers, and even buses. However, the company also built a number of Woodies on Armstrong Siddeley, Riley, and even war surplus Humber chassis.

Castle Bodies

This company built bodies which were high on styling, but seemingly low on quality. Both Alvis and Lea-Francis vehicles were bodied.

Gaze

Only two Lea-Francis Woodies are recorded as being bodied by Gaze Ltd of Kingston-on-Thames, but the

This Riley RM is one of two bodied by Bonallack. It is notable for having fastback styling.

The body builders

Gaze Ltd of Kingston-on-Thames bodied this 1947 Alvis TA14. (Courtesy John Colley)

The body builders

Frank Grounds of Aston bodied this stylish little Austin A40 commercial-based Woodie.

This two-cylinder Bradford CB is seen here in 1948 receiving its first coat of paint in the workshops of Frank Grounds.

British Woodies from the 1920s to the 1950s

exact same style of bodywork was used by Gaze on many of the Alvis TA14 chassis it bodied, a number of which survive to this day.

Frank Grounds

The origins of this company stretch back to 1894 when a horse-drawn cartage business was established. Frank Grounds quickly took control of the company and acquired its first motor truck. In 1926, Richards Bodybuilders of Aston, Birmingham, which was building truck bodies for the company, was also acquired. So, while the transport and body building business flourished, Frank P Grounds Ltd (FPG) branched out into used car sales, and, in 1934, became a dealer for new Morris cars and commercials. FPG became Jowett main agents in 1946, and acquired a number of 'driveaway chassis' on which it could mount its own bodywork.

Like many other companies, during the immediate post-war years, FPG bodied any chassis it could get its hands on in order to meet the demand for new, car-sized vehicles. Austin, Alvis, and Armstrong Siddeley models were firm favourites for converting to shooting brakes, and FPG also turned out a number of vans, trucks – and even milk float bodies.

Hooper

London-based Hooper was probably one of the companies least likely to be associated with building shooting brakes. With a reputation for being the best coachbuilder in Britain, the company had experimented

Humber Pullman with Hooper bodywork.

Jennings of Sandbach constructed this bus-sized Woodie on an ex-military, 1940 Canadian Ford chassis.

with aluminium framing before the war, and, from 1949 on, its car bodywork was produced almost entirely with aluminium framing. Except for a few Woodies, of course!

Jennings

Jennings Brothers of Sandbach had a long and illustrious career building a great variety of bodies for commercial vehicles. Starting in the 1920s with truck bodies for Fords, the company grew and prospered, and, despite a number of different businesses formed by different Jennings brothers, the Jennings name is perhaps most famously connected with the fibreglass truck cabs that it

Standard 8 with bodywork by Jennings of Sandbach.

Austin FL1 bodied by Jennings of Sandbach.

The body builders

designed and built for truck builder, ERF, also located in Sandbach.

Jennings capitalised on the post-war boom in shooting brakes and bodied a number of Austin A70 commercial chassis, FL1 hire car chassis, and a small number of ex-military Fords.

Jensen-bodied Alvis TA14.

Jensen

Birmingham-based Jensen began life as a coachbuilding firm, back in 1928, before becoming a vehicle manufacturer in its own right. At least one 1936 Jensen-Ford V8 Woodie was built, followed by a small number of Ford 10HP Woodies. After World War II, the company also constructed utility bodywork on Alvis and Lea-Francis chassis.

Jones Brothers

West London-based Jones Brothers rebodied a number of Rolls-Royce chassis with utility bodywork. The

British Woodies from the 1920s to the 1950s

company also clothed a large number of Alvis TA14s with sleek utility bodywork.

Mulliner

Birmingham-based Mulliner manufactured bodywork for a number of chassis builders, and is known to have produced a number of shooting brakes based on Lanchester and Standard vehicles.

The compact post-war Standard 8 was an ideal base for a small, but perfectly formed Woodie. This example is believed to have been bodied by Mulliner of Birmingham.

Papworth Industries

Cambridgeshire-based Papworth Industries had not bodied a single

This rare shot shows a stripped down Austin A70 saloon just after it had been driven from Austin's Longbridge Works to Papworth for conversion to a Woodie Countryman. Apparently, four or five cars would be delivered together to Papworth, their drivers travelling back to Longbridge in a support car. Health & Safety obviously wasn't such a big concern in the 1950s ...

vehicle before winning the contract from Austin, in 1947, to build 250 500 Austin 16 Countryman Woodies. The quality of the finished work was on a par with that of the best coachbuilders in the UK, which did not go unnoticed: Austin ordered a further 250 Woodies. It seems likely that the Countryman name was born with the Austin 16 Woodie, as, whilst an early brochure describes it as a shooting brake, the most common version of the same brochure has the model as the Countryman.

The Austin A70-based BW3 Countryman that followed in 1949 was much more modern and stylish

The body builders

The Austin A70 Hereford Countryman production line at Papworth Industries. Four-door saloon car bodies are being cut down and modified to accept wooden bodywork.

than contemporary Alvis, Ford and Lea-Francis models. It created quite a stir when introduced, but, with almost 90 per cent of the 900 vehicles produced going for export, it also created a void. London-based Austin dealer, Car Mart Ltd, capitalised on this by acquiring 200 of the readily available A70 Hampshire pickup chassis cabs from Longbridge, and shipping them to Papworth to be built into copies of the BW3 Countryman. Papworth designated these vehicles as simply 'Brakes,' and, although not exact copies of the BW3, it is doubtful if the new, car-starved market in the UK cared, or even noticed.

Whilst wooden body construction meant a reduction in steel, the BW3 Countryman retained the saloon's

Papworth Industries also built a prototype Austin A40 Woodie, but Austin never put it into production, preferring instead to stick side windows in its A40 van and call it a Countryman.

British Woodies from the 1920s to the 1950s

steel front doors. Surviving Papworth workers, including the chief pattern maker that I tracked down, have never explained the reason for this, although I suspect it must have been something to do with how to effectively marry wood to the sweeping curves of the A70's front wings. By using steam presses to bend and shape wooden panels, Chrysler managed this very effectively with its Town & Country Woodie convertibles of the late 1940s, but this was an elaborate process probably not available on this side of the Atlantic.

The A70 Hampshire was replaced by the Hereford at the end of 1950, and, within a few months, the Austin BW4 Countryman Woodie had been designed and was being built at Papworth. The earlier problems experienced with building 'curvy' front doors had been overcome, and the BW4 went on to become the most popular of all Austin Woodie: more than 1500 were built up until the A70 went out of production at the end of 1954, replaced by the unitary construction Austin A90 Westminster.

Papworth Industries obviously relished its new-found role as a car builder, and began to experiment with building estate cars for other manufacturers. In 1954 it bodied two Lea-Francis 14HP shooting brakes, one of which was to appear at the Earls Court Motor Show; just a few years earlier it had built a prototype metal-bodied estate car on the then-new Ford Zephyr for the Ford Motor Company. While the last Woodie to roll out of the Papworth factory did so in 1954, the company continued in the commercial vehicle industry by building TV outside broadcast units, took on sub-contract work

Bentley-based Radford Countryman.

The body builders

Bentley MkVI with bodywork by persons unknown.

This 1952 Bentley R-type was bodied as a shooting brake from new by John Jackson & Sons of Dunfermline. Apart from building van and truck bodies, this company also built Woodie bodies on Austin FX3 chassis.

British Woodies from the 1920s to the 1950s

for Duple, and eventually built a number of the legendary 'Green Goddess' fire appliances for the Ministry of Defence.

J Urquhart & Son

Founded in Petersfield in 1922, J Urquhart & Son took the traditional route of evolving first from a garage concern into road haulage, and then into coachbuilding. As a main dealer for Bedford vehicles, the company specialised in a one hundred pound conversion of a Bedford van to a utility, but also built a number of shooting brake bodies on Austin, Alvis and Riley chassis.

Whitacres

Whitacres Coachbuilders of Stoke-on-Trent was founded in 1947, and located in the former British Railways stables at the disused Hanley station.

The company undertook the conversion to shooting brakes of numerous production van and light commercial chassis, including a number of Austin A70 Hampshire and Hereford-based chassis cabs. It also bodied a number of smaller Austin A40 Devon shooting brakes and utility vans – the latter without side glass to avoid paying purchase tax.

One of the most interesting models to roll out of the Hanley factory was the prototype Standard 8 Woodie, which was built as a possible rival to the newly-launched Morris Minor Traveller. Sadly, this was not taken up by Standard Motors and the car has long-since disappeared. However, a replica of this lost prototype is now being recreated for a Standard enthusiast with a little help from former Whitacres employees.

Willenhall Coachcraft

This company's roots can be traced back to building ambulances during World War II, and then constructing coach and bus bodies in the post-war period. Like many other coachbuilders, Willenhall Coachcraft quickly realised that there was great opportunity in re-bodying war surplus vehicles, and so acquired many ex-military Humber, Standard, Morris, and Austin vehicles to convert to Woodies. One of Willenhall's notable achievements was re-bodying war surplus Jeeps as Woodies; of the 80 to 90 conversions carried out, at least one is known to survive.

J Urquhart of Petersfield bodied a number of utility vehicles, including the Riley RM, Austin A70, and this Alvis TA14.

Whitacres of Stoke-on-Trent employed a lot of style and flair when building Woodies, such as this Austin A70, commercial-based example.

Austin A40 commercial chassis bodied by Whitacres.

British Woodies from the 1920s to the 1950s

The body builders

Inset, left: Whitacres bodywork on an Austin A70 Hereford-based commercial chassis.

Left: A number of Austin FL1 hire car chassis received shooting brake bodies, including this example which was later rebuilt by Whitacres.

This Austin FL1 has the spare wheel mounted externally to maximise passenger space.

One of the most attractively-proportioned of the FL1 Woodies is this example, with bodywork by an unknown builder.

A great many small coachbuilders used the A70 commercial chassis cab as the basis for building Woodies. This example, by persons unknown, has planked sides and looks very utilitarian.

1950 Morris Y-type utility by unknown coachbuilder.

This mighty Humber Pullman carries what is described as a 'utility body' by Wilson & Stockall of Bury.

Beginning of the end

The British car building industry has a long and rich history of change, evolution, and development, and, whilst a number of factors contributed to the wooden-bodied shooting brake being built in the 1920s, a great many more contributed to its eventual demise.

Coachbuilt wooden-framed bodies had always been labour-intensive to build. They neatly filled a niche market in the early post-war years, but rising labour and materials costs meant that they became more expensive to build. They also required a high level of maintenance – the average recommended period between major re-varnishing was just two years if a decent level of weather protection for the wood was to be achieved. Needless to say, most owners didn't carry out this work, which drastically shortened woodwork life; ten years was the best that could be expected before it suffered serious structural integrity problems.

There are several recorded instances of vehicles being returned to builders within the first two years of use for replacement of plywood panels which were delaminating. Woodies that were exported to tough overseas markets – as so many were – fared even worse, as many were literally shaken to pieces on unmade roads.

Woodie construction used traditional coachbuilding techniques, which usually entailed plywood flat side panels. However, some coachbuilders experimented with aluminium flat panels in place of wood, and some went even further and clad the entire shooting brake bodywork in aluminium panels in exactly the same way that van bodies were built.

This Alvis, bodied by Jennings of Sandbach, shows how new, streamlined designs could be created using aluminium panelling.

This 1950 Armstrong Siddeley began life as a Station coupé; in essence a four-seater pickup truck. It was later converted to an all-metal utility vehicle.

Beginning of the end

One of the new generation, all-aluminium estate cars built by Hooper. Sadly, in terms of survival, they didn't fare any better than those with wooden bodies.

While shooting brakes, estate cars, and station wagons were certainly not mainstream vehicles in the 1930s and 40s, some car makers had begun to take note of them, and made plans to introduce their own version to neatly fill gaps in model ranges. With sleek modern post-war car designs bearing more than a passing resemblance to the aircraft-inspired designs rolling out of Detroit, exterior woodwork was beginning to look a little old-fashioned.

Some car makers hedged their bets by introducing a second tier estate car range, which gave an indication of where the market was going. While many Austin

British Woodies from the 1920s to the 1950s

Using steel-bodied pickup trucks as the basis for a 'cheap and cheerful utility' vehicle – such as this Papworth-modified Austin A70 – helped vehicle manufacturers move toward manufacture of the metal-bodied estate car.

This prototype Standard 8 Woodie was built by Whitacres to compete with the Morris Minor Traveller. It never went into production as Standard introduced the steel-bodied Companion estate car instead.

1955 Morris Oxford Traveller series II. This example sports wooden side panels, cleverly placed over the standard metal panels.

British Woodies from the 1920s to the 1950s

A40-based commercial chassis were being converted to Woodies by independent coachbuilders, Austin surprised everybody in 1948 with the launch of its own A40 Countryman – based on the metal-bodied van bodyshell. The same year the all-steel Standard Vanguard estate car was introduced: not to be outdone, the Nuffield Group introduced the Morris Y-type van-based utility, converted for the car maker by Martin Walter of Folkestone under the brand name Utilecon.

However, whereas all of these individual circumstances might have eventually brought about the inevitable, the main reason for the demise of the Woodie was progress. After decades of building vehicles with separate chassis and bodies, in the early 1950s the British motor industry was increasingly moving over to the mass-production of unitary construction cars, and this, more than anything else, finally killed off the coachbuilt Woodie.

Sales of Woodies had never been high, especially when compared to the volumes achieved by saloon cars, and when purchase tax was applied to commercial vehicles for the first time in April 1950, some manufacturers saw sales fall even further. Both Alvis and Lea-Francis were hard hit, though Austin soldiered on until 1954 when the last separate chassis A70 Countryman rolled off the production line.

The 1956 Morris Isis Traveller was the last big UK mass-produced Woodie. It was available with extra seats in the back, making it a seven-seater, but it really could have done with four doors. Today, it's a real rarity.

Restoring for tomorrow

Apart from a handful of Alvis, Austin, Ford, and Lea-Francis shooting brakes – and not forgetting a few hundred surviving Morris Minor Travellers – most of the surviving Woodies in the UK are unique. As mentioned previously, the combination of exposed wooden framework and the need for regular re-varnishing meant that most Woodies met with an untimely end.

Stories abound of elderly Woodies being held together with bailing wire, string, and even threaded steel bars with nuts at both ends. In 2005 I purchased a set of wooden side doors from a long-scrapped, Papworth-bodied Austin 16 Countryman, and was astonished to discover a combination of angle iron, threaded bar, and sheet steel neatly screwed inside the wooden frames. This commingle was, in effect, the only thing holding the doors together, as woodworm had long since devoured the tenons.

With so many different designs and body styles during the heyday of the British Woodie, it's a shame that so few survive to remind us of the golden age of British coachbuilding. As numerous cars were bodied in small batches by companies, and sometimes individuals,

Unique Jaguar Foxbat built in the 1970s was a marriage between a rusty Jaguar X150, rescued from a scrapyard, and the back half of a Morris Minor Traveller.

This Jones-bodied Alvis TA14 has been rescued from a farm in Cornwall, and is now undergoing a total restoration.

The sad remains of an Armstrong Siddeley 346 Woodie that had lain in a Norfolk field for 14 years. This car has now been rescued, pending restoration.

This Austin A70 Countryman looked to be on its last legs when photographed for sale in the late 1980s, but it has undergone a major restoration and could soon be back on the road.

British Woodies from the 1920s to the 1950s

This 1948 Bristol 400 was bodied by Hereford coachbuilder, F J Hyde, to the order of Mr Parry, a local butcher. Seems he had visited the London Motor Show and was impressed with the new Bristol, but was unable to purchase a complete car due to the long waiting list for non-essential buyers. He acquired a chassis from Bristol at Filton and had it bodied to suit his tastes. When initially completed it had wood panels where the side windows should be, and no rear seat to enable it to be registered as a van and avoid a purchase tax bill of more than £800. While currently looking rather sad, it is in the process of being restored and will be a rare sight indeed when it returns to British roads.

of which there is no trace, it's no wonder that many of the surviving Woodies have no record of who built them.

The Woodie Car Club was formed in 2000, with the aim of creating a knowledge base to help owners with the restoration and preservation of coachbuilt Woodies in the UK. Owners of Morris Minor Travellers are fortunate enough – by virtue of the large number of surviving cars – to be able to use the services of numerous specialists that can supply everything from a single piece of ash framing to a completely new body.

Owners of coachbuilt cars, on the other hand, find that they have to enlist the services of specialist

Restoring for tomorrow

This 1934 Ford Model Y was converted to utility bodywork by persons unknown. It is awaiting restoration in the north of England.

British Woodies from the 1920s to the 1950s

This 1929 Rolls-Royce 20HP was originally bodied by Hoyal, but some time in its life acquired this utility body supplied by Radford. It is now being restored by Clanfield Coachbuilding.

coachbuilders to remake everything from scratch. Most of the surviving Woodies now seem to fall into two categories: restored or nice original cars, or basket cases that need the help of a skilled craftsman if they are ever going to return to the road.

While many home restorers have basic engineering and metal-bashing skills, most find the prospect of working with hard woods such as ash, oak, and maple a daunting prospect. The Woodie Car Club acts as an information exchange on restoration techniques and processes for owners of Woodies, and has also been able to help owners find professional help from companies such as Clanfield Coachbuilding. However, as interest in Woodies grows, so enthusiasts are taking on more and more adventurous restoration projects, and finding that there is an acute shortfall in the number of coachbuilders able to rebuild these old gems on a timely and cost-effective basis.

The Woodie Car Club can be contacted via its website: www.woodiecarclub.com.

Also from Veloce Publishing –

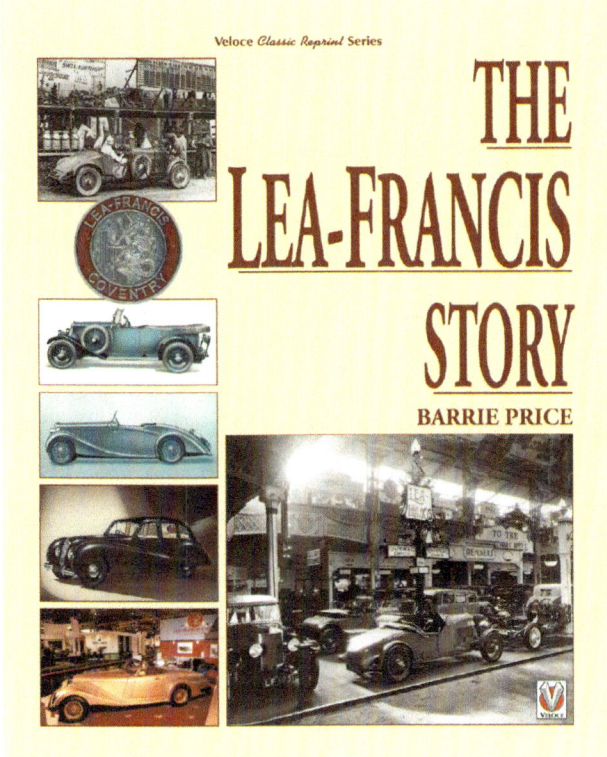

ISBN 9781845849573

ISBN 9781787114739

*prices subject to change. p&p extra; please call 01305 260068/visit www.veloce.co.uk for details

Also from Veloce Publishing –

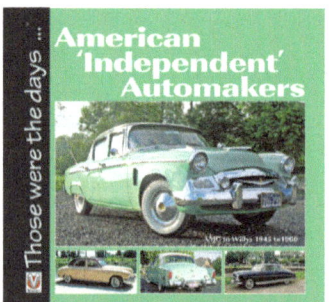

ISBN 9781845842390

ISBN 9781845842642

ISBN 9781845843694

ISBN 9781787111158

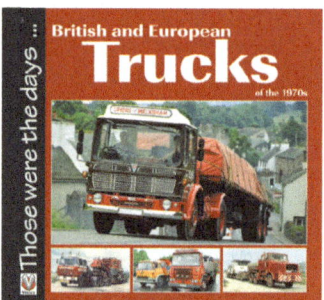

ISBN 9781845844158

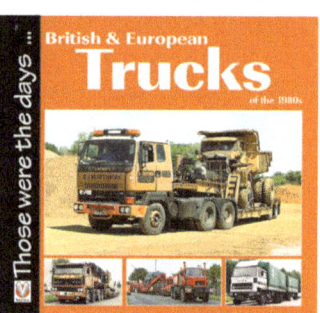

ISBN 9781845844172

ISBN 9781845844608

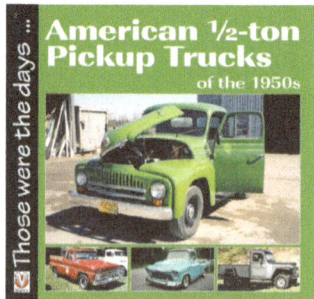

ISBN 9781845848026

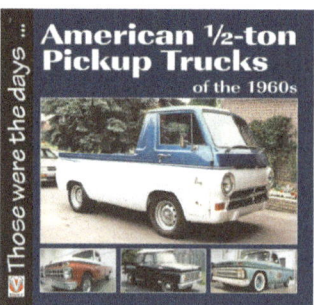

ISBN 9781845848033

ISBN 9781787111127

ISBN 9781787111134

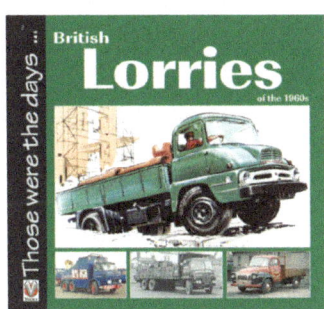

ISBN 9781787111141

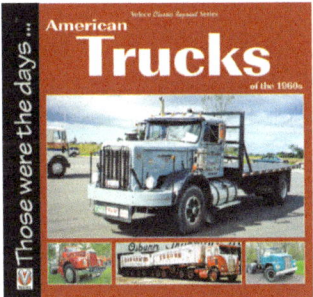

ISBN 9781787111721

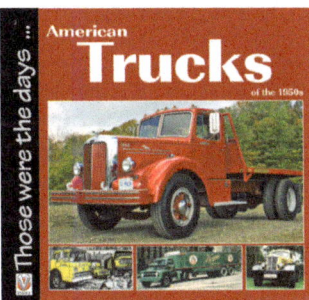

ISBN 9781787112643

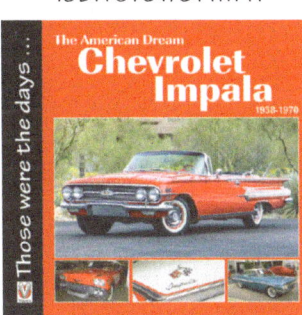

ISBN 9781787113107

ISBN 9781787113565

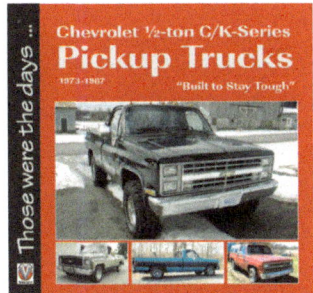

ISBN 9781787113114

– with more to come!

Also from Veloce Publishing –

9781787110960

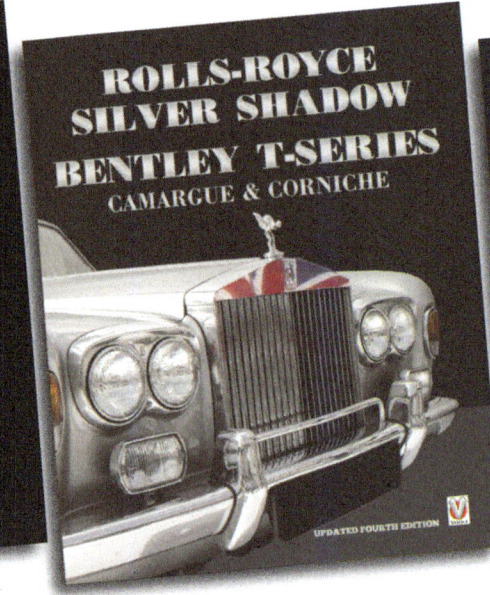

9781787111370

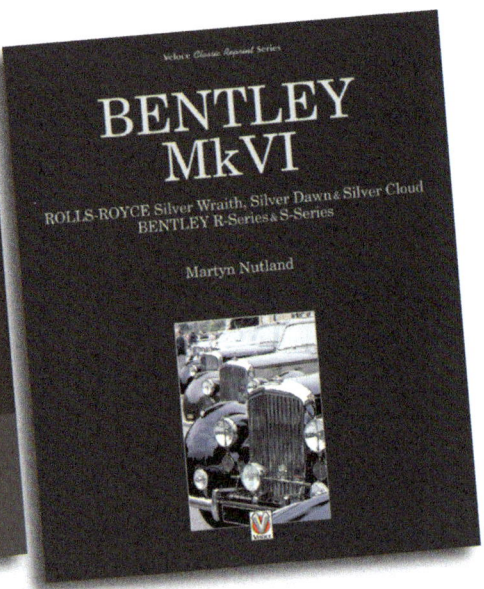

9781845840686

9781845841010

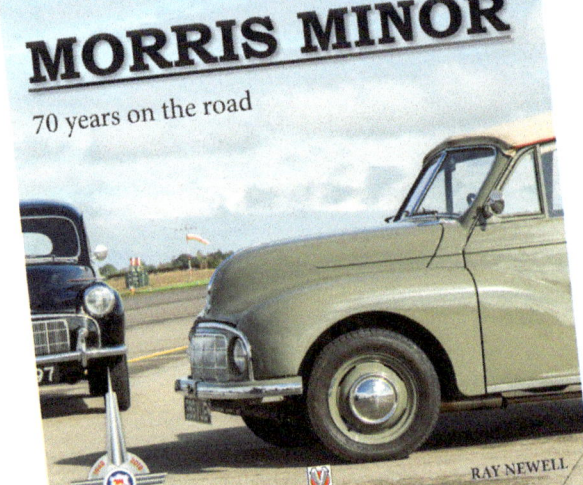

9781787112070

*prices subject to change. p&p extra; please call 01305 260068/visit www.veloce.co.uk for details

Index

AC Cars 56
AP Aircraft 19
Allard 37
Alvis 19, 37, 56, 60, 65, 72, 79, 86
Alvis 12/50 8
Alvis Silver Eagle 8
Angel Motor Bodies 58
Armstrong Siddeley 80, 87
Associated Coachcraft 57
Austin A40 22, 61, 69, 73
Austin A70 19, 40, 41, 67-69, 73, 74, 76, 81, 82, 87
Austin FL1 64, 74-76
Austin Sixteen 18, 19, 40
Austin Ten 9

Bentley 34, 35, 70
Blitz Buggy 33
Bonallack 58
Bradford 61
Bristol 88
Brooklands of Bond Street 56

Car Mart 19
Castle Bodies 58
Clanfield Coachbuilding 90
Commer 12, 13

Daimler 21

Dex Garages 9

Ford Model A 7
Ford Model Y 89
Ford Pilot 15, 46-47
Ford V8 8, 29-33, 42-44, 63
Fordson 14

Gaze 39, 56, 58, 60
Grounds, Frank 61, 62

Hooper 62, 81
Humber Pullman 62, 78
Humber Super Snipe 23, 25-28
Hyde, F J 88

Invicta 57

Jackson, John 71
Jaguar 83
Jeep 35, 36
Jennings of Sandbach 63, 64, 79
Jensen 65
Jones Brothers 65, 86

Kevill Davies 12
Kidd Brothers 35

Lanchester 10 6
Lea-Francis   9, 17, 19, 42, 48, 50, 51

MG VA 11
Morris Isis 84
Morris Minor Traveller 54
Morris Oxford Traveller 52, 53, 82, 83
Morris Y-type 77
Mulliner 6, 66

Nash of Southampton 6

Packard 11, 34
Papworth Industries 18, 19, 40, 66-70, 82

Radford 70, 71, 90
Remploy 34
Riley RM 20, 58, 59
Rolls-Royce 20hp 5, 90

Rolls-Royce 20/25hp 6, 35
Rolls-Royce Phantom 5

Standard 8 64, 66, 82
Standard 12 24, 34
Standard 14 16
Studebaker Studex 9

Thrupp & Maberley 23

University Motors 11
Urquhart, J 72

Wallis & Co 35
Whitacres 72-73, 82
Willenhall Coachcraft 72
Wilson & Stockall 78
Wolseley 25 10

Visit Veloce on the web: www.veloce.co.uk
Information on all books • New book news • Special offers • Gift vouchers